GETTING IN TOUCH
W I T H Y O U R
INNER BITCH

AIRPORT BRISBANE 3/96

GETTING IN TOUCH WITH YOUR INNER BITCH

by

ELIZABETH HILTS

Thorsons
An Imprint of HarperCollins*Publishers*

Thorsons
An Imprint of HarperCollins*Publishers*
77–85 Fulham Palace Road,
Hammersmith, London W6 8JB

First published in the USA
by Hysteria Publications 1994
Published by Thorsons 1995
1 3 5 7 9 10 8 6 4 2

A catalogue record for this book
is available from the British Library

ISBN 0 7225 3211 3

Printed in Great Britain by
HarperCollinsManufacturing Glasgow

Quotations in this book come from the following sources:
The Beacon Book of Quotations by Women, compiled by Rosalie Maggio,
    Beacon Press, 1992;
Familiar Quotations, compiled by John Bartlett, edited by Emily Morrison
    Beck, Little, Brown & Co., 1980;
GlibQuips: Funny Words by Funny Women, edited by Roz Warren,
    The Crossing Press, 1994;
The Last Word, edited by Caroline Warner, Prentice Hall, 1992;
The MacMillan Dictionary of Quotations, edited by the Bloomsbury Press
    Staff, MacMillan, 1989.

DEDICATION

This book is for my daughter, Shannon Hillory Hector, whose insight and assistance were essential elements in its completion, and for my father, Robert Gifford Hilts, whom I still miss every day.

ACKNOWLEDGEMENTS

I would like to acknowledge the following people for their part in bringing this book to fruition: Jim Motavalli (who believed in me long before I believed in myself); Mary Ann Masarech; Laura Fedele; Judith Gardner; Karen Drena; Piper Machette; Richard Howe; my fairy godmother, Jocelyn K. Moreland; Felicia and David Robinson (who gave me shelter in the early stages of this book); Jeff Yoder; Tom Connor; Sarah Waite and Lysbeth Guillorn for research and editing; cartoonists Nicole Hollander, Marian Henley, and Mary Lawton; Mace Norwood, who was right all those years ago; and all my beloved friends who are just too wonderful (and too numerous) to mention by name.

Very special thanks to Deborah Werksman for her extreme patience, consistent kindness, boundless enthusiasm and, above all, her gentle honesty and acumen.

/ COULD YOU TAKE
ON MORE WORK
WITHOUT A RAISE
OR A NEW title?

/ I'D LIKE YOU TO
CALL MORE OFTEN.

— WOULD YOU MAKE
12 DOZEN BISCUITS
FOR the
Fête... SORRY it's
SUCH SHORT NOTICE.

CONTENTS

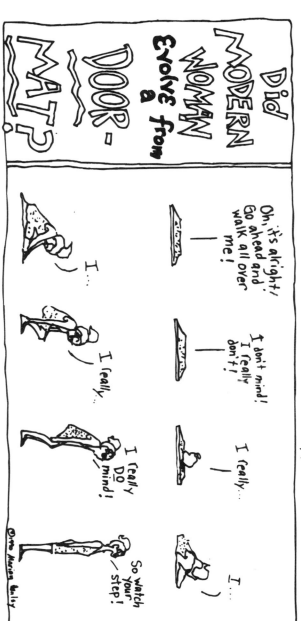

STOOD UP;
WISED UP

**'We had a lot in common.
I loved him. And he loved him.'**
Shelley Winters

Let me take a few moments to explain why I wrote this book.

It started in February 1993 with my article, 'Get in Touch with Your Inner Bitch', published in *Hysteria*, the humour magazine for women.

The magazine came out, a radio personality saw the article and called me for an interview, and suddenly I was deemed the Expert on the Inner Bitch.

Well, I am. But before I became the Expert on Her, I was an expert on the topic of Toxic Niceness. I was trained from the day of my birth in the ways of being Nice. The first thing my mother ever said to me was 'Elizabeth, behave.'

And I tried. Honestly. I attempted to be a paragon of Niceness – a Melanie Wilkes, a Beth (from *Little Women*) or was it Amy?), a Nancy Drew. I memorized the names of that most toxic family, the Nicelys – Act, Speak, Sit, Think, even Dress.

Speak Nicely was tough. I tried to keep my voice low and well modulated. When that didn't work, I pushed it a full octave higher, which forced me to whisper. I thought I sounded sweet. Everyone else thought I had laryngitis.

Dress Nicely nearly pushed me to the edge. Dress Nicely, when I wanted halter tops. Décolletage! Spandex!

But in the end, it was old Act Nicely that was the most toxic of the Nicelys for me. I simply couldn't do it. I laughed too loudly; I spoke my mind. When I was a teenager, my girlfriends would say, 'Stop making a spectacle of yourself!'

If extreme discretion was called for, they would nudge my arm and hiss, 'Liiiiiiz!'

In private, they shrieked with laughter as they recounted the story of my latest outrageous behaviour.

Besides, we all knew the truth: It was the bitches who got all the good stuff. I mean, Scarlett O'Hara was the star of the movie, wasn't she? And she got the sequel. Melanie may have had Ashley, but who wanted Ashley? Anyone with eyes could see that Ashley was – Ashley.

But the scales of Niceness remained over my eyes.

Until IT happened. The event that finally made me see that Niceness could be toxic.

The Moment of Truth

It had to do with a man. In my case, that phrase can be followed with the addendum, 'of course'. This is acutely embarrassing to tell you, but I know I must. Here's what happened: I got stood up.

Yes. Left sitting in my living room on a Saturday night. After I'd tried on and rejected five different (fabulous) outfits. I called his house, got his machine. Left a message. 'Hi, it's nearly 9:00. You must be running late. See you when you get here.' 9:15, 9:45. I went upstairs at 10:30, took off my makeup, and got into bed, where I tossed and turned from concern to anger and back again all night.

He called the next day with some feeble excuse. 'You understand, don't you?'

Of course I did. I understood completely. But I forgave him anyway because he was really cute, and I really liked him. And because no one likes a bitch. How could a nice girl like me stay angry? He asked for another chance and I gave it to him.

You know it had to happen again. And this time, I went ballistic! I called his answering machine, ranting and raving until the tape ran out. Then I called back to yell some more. Finally, on the third go-round, I was all yelled out and the old training kicked in. 'I'm really sorry, but I am really hurt,' I whispered hoarsely into the phone. 'Please call me.'

Did you see that? Did you see what I did there? I can't believe it myself. I apologized! I told his answering machine I was hurt! I wasn't hurt, I was furious! But, you know, he *was* cute, and I thought I could, maybe, *really* like him, and he'd never treat me so badly if he knew what a Nice Girl I was.

On the count of three: 'Oh, come on!'

YES! And when I realized what I'd done, I decided right then and there that it was time to give up Toxic Niceness. It was time to emulate the bitches of the world. I would, as my mother would say, take a page from their book.

But there was no book.
Until now.

Maxine
The Excitement!
MISS HONESTY's sure got a well-developed conscience!
CLAP!
But MISS WISDOM has a perfect perspective!
CLAP! CLAP!
You won't believe MISS INTELLIGENCE's measurements! Her I.Q. is 210 and...
The Talent!
For the talent competition, MISS COMPASSION will take the weight of the world on her shoulders!
CLAP! CLAP! CLAP!
The Glamour!
For evening wear, MISS SACRIFICE chooses overalls and a bandanna for those nights spent volunteering in soup kitchens!
"CLAP! CLAP! CLAP!
Who could possibly win the title?
Miss Inner Beauty Pageant
I hope someone other than ME wins!
I don't DESERVE to win!
I think EVERYONE should win!
THE JUDGES HAVE REACHED THEIR DECISION!
No one has the right to judge others!
MISS GENEROSITY
MISS MODESTY
MISS COMMUNITY
MISS FAIRNESS
They're all just too beautiful!
CLAP! CLAP! CLAP! CLAP!
©1990 Marian Henley

1 TOXIC NICENESS

'No woman is all sweetness.'
Mme. Récamier

Toxic Niceness is what happens to us after we internalize the Nicely Family. Toxic Niceness is like yeast. Yeast causes dough to become nice and light. Toxic Niceness causes us to try and make life nice and light. For everyone else. We who suffer from Toxic Niceness work hard to make things a little sweeter, using our own personal 'sugar' to make lemonade out of life's lemons. Far too often, this is achieved at a terrible cost to ourselves.

The fact that you are reading this is proof that you are willing to let go of Toxic Niceness. Are you a long-time sufferer of the syndrome? Ask yourself these questions:

1 Have you ever wanted to give someone a piece of your mind and eaten a piece of cake instead?
2 How about the whole cake?
3 Have you ever said, 'I don't know what came over me!'?
4 Have you ever refused an invitation because you were

waiting for the newest apple of your eye to ask you out on Saturday night?

5 Have you ever sat at home alone on Saturday night because the newest apple of your eye never called?

6 Have you ever said 'yes' when you meant 'I don't think so'?

7 Do you apologize a lot?

8 Have you ever worn a bridesmaid's dress with spaghetti straps?

If you answered yes to any of these questions, it's a sure thing that you're using too much sugar. But all is not lost – take heart. Toxic Niceness need not be a problem any longer.

Your Inner Bitch awaits you. Read on.

SYLVIA
by Nicole Hollander.

PRotective

INCONSIDeRate

2 MEET YOUR INNER BITCH

'Until you've lost your reputation you never realize what a burden it was, or what freedom really is.'
Margaret Mitchell

There is a powerful and integral part of each of us that has until now gone unrecognized, its energy largely untapped. Years of repression have sent this aspect of ourselves into hiding in the nooks and crannies of our souls. Because we misunderstand it, we do all we can to keep it in the dark where we believe it belongs.

It is the Inner Bitch. Don't pretend you don't know what I'm talking about.

We all know Her. She floats constantly just under the surface of our consciousness and our culture. She is a part of ourselves that is smart, confident, dignified, and knows what she wants. She tells us not to settle for less. She warns us as we are about to embark on self-defeating behaviour.

The Inner Bitch is not that part of ourselves that is sometimes stupid, or mean, or humourless. She neither indulges in self-defeating behaviour, nor does She abuse Herself or others.

The Inner Bitch does not engage in petty arguments, even for sport. Why bother?

The Inner Bitch never enters into a battle of wits with an unarmed opponent. And she is never afraid to say, 'Screw 'em if they can't take a joke.'

I hold this truth to be self-evident: By releasing Her, we can use Her power and energy for our own higher purposes.

If we ignore Her, we risk having her run amok when the pressure of being Nice grows too strong. We've all seen it happen; it's not a pretty sight.

When we don't acknowledge our Inner Bitch, we get pimples. Or we get fat. Or too thin, controlling, manipulative, whiny, weepy, or hysterical. We don't insist on practising safe sex.

None of this is productive. Some of it is down-right dangerous.

How do we put an end to these self-defeating behaviours, particularly after a lifetime of Toxic Niceness?

All it takes is one short phrase:

'I don't think so.'

We all think it. But we bat it away like a pesky little gnat. 'That's not nice,' we think. But, oh, the price we pay.

You may be asking yourself, 'But can I be nice without being toxic?'

Certainly you can! In fact, being in touch with your Inner Bitch actually helps you to be truly nice. There is a world of difference between being nice and being Nice.

Your Inner Bitch does not want you to be mean. She

wants you to be firm. She wants you to be reasonable. And She wants you to be kind. Particularly to yourself.

Getting to 'I Don't Think So'

Give it a shot. Start out with small increments. Think of a situation in your life where it might be applicable. For example:

☐ Your 22-year-old daughter wants to move into her old bedroom, rent-free, with her lover and his motorcycle.

You say: 'I don't think so.'

☐ The man you've been dating for a month demands in a fit of jealousy that you cancel a dinner meeting with an important client.

Your response: 'I don't think so.'

☐ Your mother wants you to meet the son of her bridge partner. 'Just a little dinner, darling. We've made reservations for you at the Four Seasons after the theatre.'

You smile: 'Mum, I don't think so.'

☐ Your boss strongly suggests that you invest your year-end bonus in his cousin's latest venture.

You: 'I don't think so.'

Saying Less, Meaning More

See? It works. No one can mistake the meaning of the phrase. Arguing against it is futile; how can anyone claim that you *do* think so if you say you don't?

It's gentle. It's polite. But it's strong, firm and indisputable.

The best thing about 'I don't think so' is that it can be used at any time during a conversation. If you catch yourself sliding into Toxic Niceness, it's very easy to break the fall. And if you forget to say it, don't worry – the opportunity is guaranteed to come up again.

Saying More

Naturally, there are times when 'I don't think so' isn't enough. It's a base upon which to build, to make a sort of verbal sundae. Heap on as many toppings as you like:

'I don't think I can lend you my great-grandmother's diamond earrings, but I have cubic zirconia that you're welcome to take.'

'I don't think I can fit that in.'

'I don't think that's a good colour for me.'

'I don't think I'm ready for that.'

Then there are those cases that require a certain delicacy combined with an ability to think on your feet:

You are at a party. A friend of a friend introduces himself to you and says, 'Do you know that Jim told me you're the perfect woman for me?' You have no interest in this man, but to be polite, you say, 'I don't think so, but hum a few bars.'

You see, the phrase is polite and reasonable, never cruel, and not hard to say. Try different tones of voice. Give it a musing tone, or try putting the emphasis on different words: I *don't* think so. I don't *think* so!

I THINK I'D LIKE
TO BE LESS OF A
SWEETIE PIE
AND MORE
OF A
BITCH.

3 | THE P.R. PROBLEM

'You only start being called bitch when you become successful.'
Judith Regan

Some of us may have a problem claiming the term 'bitch' for ourselves. We may believe that to do so would affirm the negative image assertive women have borne for years. To wit: If we say what we really think, we must be a bitch.

Let's take a close look at this issue.

What exactly is the problem here? Are we really behaving badly? Or are we just going too fast, getting too far ahead, breaking out of our designated niche?

Calling us bitch puts us on notice that it is time to beat a hasty retreat to Toxic Niceness.

All I can say is, 'I don't think so.'

Unfortunately, many of us have fallen prey to this sort of name-calling. Gather together almost any group of women and get us talking about bitchiness. We'll admit that it exists. We'll even admit that we have, on occasion, resorted to bitchy behaviour ourselves, but only if we were forced into it. In more candid moments, we'll talk about our bitchiness with gleeful pride. Because, let's face it, there have been times in all our lives when being a bitch was fun.

But ask us if we consider ourselves bitches and we will say no. Oh no, no, no, no, NO! We consider ourselves Nice Girls who are occasionally backed against the wall and must defend ourselves by acting like bitches. It's 'those other women' who really are bitches.

Again, I don't think so.

In fact, I think that this dynamic carries in it the seeds of divisiveness. A dirty little secret is that Toxic Niceness works best when we are set apart from one another, when we are divided and disrespect each other.

.What Causes this Dynamic?

This question could keep sociologists and theorists busy for years, perhaps decades. That's fine. They need some way to justify the grant money. The simple truth is this: The true cause of the P.R. problem for the Inner Bitch is fear of being called a bitch.

Let me point out something: It's only a word. Sticks and stones may break our bones, but words can never hurt us.

If I've Got the Name, I Want the Game

Any woman who succeeds at anything is going to be called a bitch. Hillary Clinton? Bitch. Gloria Steinem? Bitch. Barbra Streisand? Bitch. The list goes on and on and ....

The point is that since we can't avoid it, why don't we embrace it? We've all had this experience: At some point in time, in front of other people, we say what we really think about some issue or person or what-have-you. At some later point in time, someone tells us that, 'So-and-so really thought you were a bitch.' (If it hasn't happened yet, just keep talking – it will.)

Most of us make sure to be particularly nice to old so-and-so next time we see them. We may even go out of our way to prove that perceiving us as a bitch is not only erroneous, but downright unfair. Or we explain away all the reasons we said whatever it was we said. 'I was under a lot of stress last time we met,' or, 'Gosh, I don't know what came over me!' Or even, 'You know, I really have a bad time with PMS.'

We retreat.

What if we responded by sending so-and-so a thank-you bouquet with a little card that said, 'I really appreciate your recognition of my Inner Bitch.'

What would happen if we stopped being afraid of this one little word?

Another point that must be made, which requires a short foray into rhetoric: What do we call a man who speaks up for himself, a man who is demanding of himself and those around him, a man who behaves as any self-respecting bitch would? A success.

Who Is to Blame for This?

Well, no one. Maybe everyone. One point about the Inner Bitch is so important, however, that it must be stated in no uncertain terms:

The Inner Bitch Is Not About Blame

The Inner Bitch simply *is*, just as the sky is simply the sky, and dishes, once dirty, must be washed. There is no need to point a finger at anyone. Nor is there a reason to apologize for being in touch with Her. After all, She is the part of us that knows what we really care about and want.

She knows that we take pride in our work and that we hold ourselves and others to a certain standard.

She knows that we want our lovers to please us sexually (more about this later).

She knows that we want our friend, The Bride, to understand that wearing taffeta after the age of 12 is embarrassing.

She knows that we want the world to take the measure of our accomplishments, not of our bodies. She knows that we want to be able to say what we know, without being called names.

As long as we deny that the Inner Bitch is part of us, as long as we succumb to Toxic Niceness, we will not get what we want. We will not get what we need. And none of us will really get what is good for all of us.

4 CAN WE TALK!

'Real sisterhood [is] ... a bunch of dames in bathrobes throwing back M&Ms and making each other laugh.'
Maxine Wilkie

It doesn't really get any better than this: a bunch of women gathered together with time to talk. And what do we women do when we talk? We get to the bottom of things. It's beautiful.

We start in adolescence, when we struggle with everything. That's when we discover how insightful our friends are, how well they understand everything.

They sympathize with us about the unreasonable curfew, and the impossible history exam; they commiserate with us over the painful braces, the boy who doesn't call, and the new shirt that shrinks in the wash; and they swoon with us over our teen idols.

Once we have recovered from our teens (and most of us do, eventually), we are able to form strong, valuable friendships with other women. Our best friendships are ones in which we meet each other head on with our Inner Bitch.

As my friends and I struggle with our tendencies toward Toxic Niceness, our Inner Bitch compels us to set boundaries that keep our friendships healthy. Emotional black-mail? Betraying secrets? Nasty gossip?

I don't think so.

Friends Indeed

Is it easy for two or more women who are in touch with their Inner Bitches to be friends? I don't think so, but it's certainly more meaningful than those relationships that are based on Toxic Niceness.

The rules that govern relationships between women are so complex that the Gordian knot looks like a child's puzzle in comparison. But it's this complexity that makes friendships of this sort so very rewarding.

Our friends who are in touch with their Inner Bitch are often the most supportive, the ones to whom we turn when we feel our resolve begin to slip in the face of unreasonable bosses and impossible deadlines, the lover who suddenly stops calling, the expensive earring lost. They are the ones who remind us of the importance of our dreams and aspirations, quietly or loudly urging us forward when the path seems too steep or long.

The primary element of women's bonding is love. If we didn't love one another, we wouldn't bother telling the truth. We'd just let one another lurch from one delusion to the next, gathering up enough experience to make blues singers of all of us.

The beauty of getting in touch with our Inner Bitch is that we can then hear own own voices. The Inner Bitch knows what She knows. And She's not afraid to say it. But it is up to us to listen. The fact is, after we have had enough experience with jive, we can see it coming. And we can sometimes pull a good friend out of harm's way.

For example, when our friend's Joe breaks her heart by running off to help his buddy start a business in Hawaii, do we point out that we'd told her so? Of course not. Being in touch with our Inner Bitch requires sensitivity.

> She: 'I can't believe he left me! And to live somewhere that's warm all year, too! Maybe I should follow him.'

> You: 'Do you know how many toxic insects there are in Hawaii?'

Then we make sure to get together often to watch movies like *Thelma and Louise* or *The Lion in Winter* and order take-away food. Eventually we move on to extremely romantic films set in locations like Alaska, taking care to point out how sexy it is to find out exactly what's under that parka.

by Nicole Hollander

SYLVIA

Test your R.I.Q.*

*Relationship Intelligence Quotient

The best place to discuss your sexual dissatisfaction with your partner is:
① In the bedroom
② In a car, traveling at high speed.
③ In a crowded elevator

5 | THE BITCH IN BED

'Love me in full being.'
Elizabeth Barrett Browning

Well, the Bitch in love – really. How can we maintain the Inner Bitch in that most heady arena of life, romance? If it is true that what we seek from our love partners is intimacy, then it is vital that said partners be aware of our Inner Bitch. We can't be intimate with anyone who doesn't know and respect every aspect of our personality. The '50s proved that.

Let's face it: Romance is where Toxic Niceness is most prevalent. And where it is most dangerous, too.

Because many of us are afraid that if the ones we love *really* knew us, they wouldn't want anything to do with us. But if they don't know the real us, we live in fear that they will no longer love us if we reveal ourselves to them.

Golly, now there's a vicious cycle! Being in touch with our Inner Bitch leads the way out of that cycle.

The Toxic Way to Intimacy

It usually starts with the first date. Here's a scenario in which Toxic Niceness is at work:

> Prospective Love Partner: 'I was thinking we should see a movie.'
>
> Nice Girl: 'That sounds terrific.'

In reality, the Nice Girl hates movies and would prefer to do something more interactive, like shoot pool. But she is unwilling to say so, for fear that her date will think she's too pushy, or too demanding, or … the list goes on and on, but it always ends with fear that the man will think she's a bitch.

During that first date, the Nice Girl will undoubtedly behave as if she is actually enjoying herself, when what she really wants is a chance to get to know this guy. She will also probably thank him for a wonderful time, all the while thinking, 'If he really likes me, eventually we'll do what I want to do.'

Of course, they never do. The Nice Girl will continue to acquiesce.

The Inner Bitch Way to Intimacy

How much simpler it is when we are fearless from the start. Watch this:

> Him: 'I was thinking we should go see a movie.'

Her: 'I'd like to get to know you better. How about we go shoot some pool?'

This way, the guy has a good idea of what she wants right from the start. And there is room to compromise. She has suggested doing what she wants and left the door open for a counteroffer. This starts the prospective relationship off on an equal footing.

Of course, the man may not want to compromise. He may, indeed, be turned off by a woman who doesn't comply with every suggestion. That sort of guy will leave eventually. But that's okay, because we don't want a Love Partner like that, do we?

I don't think so!

Sex and the Inner Bitch

Okay. Take a deep breath.

This is, admittedly, one of the most sensitive areas of our lives when it comes to the Inner Bitch. Actually, sex is one of the most sensitive issues, period. Therefore, it follows that it is most important to be in touch with our Inner Bitch *before* we fall into bed with anyone. Here's why.

Selectivity

Being in touch with our Inner Bitch ensures that we will choose carefully the people with whom we share our bodies.

There are loads of us who, in the interest of being nice, have ended up sleeping with people with whom we later realized we wouldn't even want to have a cup of coffee. (Come on, you know it's true!)

The justifications? 'I didn't want to hurt his feelings.' Or, 'I don't know, it just happened.'

No need to beat ourselves up over these things. But is it necessary to continue to do this?

I don't think so.

Orgasms

Toxic Niceness can be a serious impediment to sexual satisfaction. 'I didn't want him to think I was unhappy,' the Nice Girl says, after months (or years) of unsatisfactory sex. Being in touch with our Inner Bitch ensures that we will have orgasms. Even with other people.

And we're not afraid to have them tell us what they want, either. Everyone wins when the Bitch is in bed.

Safe Sex

Being in touch with our Inner Bitch ensures that, having chosen carefully, we will not talk ourselves into believing that, by virtue of niceness, it would be impossible for our partner (or us) to have a sexually transmittable disease. Niceness does not immunize anyone.

Insisting on practising safe sex may be difficult, but consider the alternatives. So, how does the Inner Bitch broach the subject? Forthrightly, that's how.

Like this, for example:

Everything is just right, the lights are low, music is playing softly, and you've spent the entire evening testing the waters, so to speak. You come up for air, gaze into each other's eyes. Neither of you wants to break the spell of the moment, but you know you must.

'Sweetheart,' you say. 'Are there condoms in the house?'

'No, my love,' he replies. 'But you can trust me.'

'I don't think so,' you say, pulling yourself together.

If his response is, 'No, but I'll run down to the all-night chemist,' by all means, offer to drive.

And remember, we are adults now. It's okay for us to carry condoms.

6 GLORIOUS FOOD

'The effect of eating too much lettuce is soporific'
Beatrix Potter

Q 'What does the Inner Bitch make for dinner?
A. 'A choice.'

The Inner Bitch is a powerful ally to have in the ongoing struggle between our minds and our bodies. For example, my mind says 'Grains, veggies, fruit.' My body tends to say, 'Melted cheese, melted cheese, chocolate.' What role does my Inner Bitch play in all this? Voice of reason, voice of stomach.

That's right; food is the one area where even the Inner Bitch plays both sides.

The difference is that being in touch with my Inner Bitch keeps the whole thing in perspective. She allows me to honour my food cravings while remembering to maintain good health.

Does this phrase sound familiar?: 'Oh, I've been really bad!'

Of course it does, and it's not sex we're talking about.

No, we are almost always referring to something that we've eaten. Chocolate, perhaps; chips; fettucine Alfredo; if we consume anything beyond lettuce and a Diet Coke, we judge ourselves with the harshness of Calvinists. And usually condemn ourselves to several days of eating nothing but bottled spring water and the odd carrot or celery stick. This we refer to as 'being good'.

But the question must be posed: Is it good to be cranky and light-headed?

I don't think so!

How can we think and act in our best interest when we're obsessed by calorie counts, bathroom scales and tape measures?

Back to Basics

Our Inner Bitch reminds us that food is basic to survival, not to mention peace of mind. Sometimes, food is just plain comforting. What could be better after a really wretched day than a big bowl of garlic mashed potatoes? Or an entire bag of peanut M&Ms? It may be that our Inner Bitch could have prevented us from having a wretched day in the first place, but once it's happened, our Inner Bitch knows that any means of saving a day from being a total wipeout is a good thing.

Food can also be an event, an opportunity to make contact with the important people in our lives.

Some of us find the process of getting and preparing food calming and creative. Some of us go to great lengths to avoid everything but its consumption. It doesn't really matter where you are on the spectrum, because the mechanics of food aren't the issue. What *is* the issue is that food must be dealt with. And our Inner Bitch allows us to make food arrangements that work for us.

When we are in touch with our Inner Bitch, we don't have to create a 10-course meal for in-laws who have never been kind to us, or for business associates who don't support us, or for friends with a tin palate.

Perhaps the most important point is this: Our Inner Bitch takes food, and all the rituals surrounding food, seriously. But She is not taken in by the tyrannies of fashion. What does our Inner Bitch have to say about diets that require a grown woman to consume fewer calories than a two-year-old?

'I don't think so.'

What is Her response to the expectation that all women – no matter what their natural body type – should wear clothing no larger than size 12?

'I don't think so.'

Our Inner Bitch sees the absurdity of trying to look like someone else, when each of us is already such a beauty.

7 | DAILY LIFE

'It is only trifles that irritate my nerves.'
Queen Victoria

We may think of our Inner Bitch only in connection with special occasions, sort of like a party dress or lipstick. Our thoughts might go something like this: 'I'll just save my Inner Bitch for when I really need Her. After all, I wouldn't want to wear Her out.' As if the Inner Bitch were a pair of cheap shoes with flimsy soles. Could something this powerful be so fragile?

I don't think so.

The Inner Bitch is perfect for every occasion – casual, formal, private or public – sort of like basic black. She is a vital part of our daily lives.

It is necessary, however, to practise discernment when utilizing Her power.

Knowing the Difference

There are always going to be things about which we can do nothing – traffic, queues at the supermarket, increased activity on the surface of the Sun. Do we rant and rave at these things?

I don't think so.

We can take some comfort from the knowledge that we have no power over some situations – the Inner Bitch doesn't bother expending energy on things that are beyond Her control.

At the same time, it would take a saint not to react to the pressure caused by those things that are out of our control. And maybe not reacting is a sign of Toxic Niceness. Be that as it may, the important thing to remember is that the Inner Bitch can help us to respond, rather than react, to situations that are out of our control.

Making 'I Don't Think So' Work for Us

Take a typical day. We step out every morning to conduct our lives and something happens. Something always happens. We are queueing at the deli for our bagel (lightly toasted, with just a bit of cream cheese), and when the person behind the counter asks who is next, someone steps in front of us, saying, 'I am,' and begins ordering from a list – typed single-spaced on a sheet of legal paper.

We go shopping at the mall. As we enter the up-market department store, we encounter the ubiquitous purveyor of perfumes standing at the ready with her atomizer and well-rehearsed spiel about how this scent will change our lives. 'Would you care to experience *Raison d'Être?*' she asks.

Perhaps we encounter another driver in a car park.

The type of encounter in which that driver backs into our passenger side. The impact of the collision dislodges the wing mirror, an inconvenience that (according to the other driver) will have little impact on our lives. 'The rearview mirror's all ya really need anyway, sweetie,' says he.

To each of these situations we can respond, 'I don't think so.'

This takes some practise. At first, the prospect of a direct confrontation may fill us with dread. But practice does indeed make for proficiency. And most people respond rather well to hearing the Inner Bitch mantra spoken aloud.

'Excuse me,' we say to the queue jumper. 'I don't think so. I believe I was here first.'

'*Raison d'Être?* I don't think so.' It may be necessary to shield ourselves in some way from the shower of perfume that inevitably follows fast on the heels of the offer.

'I don't think so. I want your insurance information,' we say to our new buddy.

What can they say in response, really? Is anyone going to argue?

Well, certainly there is a percentage of the population that will argue. There are plenty of people who hurl themselves into a perfectly absurd defence of just the sort of indefensible behaviour referred to here.

Do we shrink in the face of this phenomenon?

I don't think so.

The mantra of the Inner Bitch is especially helpful when we are presented with unreasonable estimates for minor car repairs, when we are asked to 'please hold' for the umpteenth time, and when others attempt to bully us into doing things for them.

Indeed, the phrase, 'I don't think so,' becomes more powerful the more we say it.

SYLVIA
by Nicole Hollander
the Woman who Worries about Everything drops the Ball and Look what almost Happened.
I'M NOT PERFECT.
4-29
©1993 BY NICOLE HOLLANDER
I GOT VERY BUSY
AND I FORGOT RUSSIA.
HONEY, I'M GLAD YOU'RE BACK ON THE JOB.
Nicole Hollander

8 | PERSONAL POLITICS

'A woman's place is in the House, the Senate, and the Oval Office.'

Anonymous

The major concern of our Inner Bitch is, naturally, our life. Just getting through the day takes so much energy that there's very little left over for anything else. Laundry? It has to get done, so we do it. Sleep? We'd die without it. Work? Well, our survival often depends on our ability to provide for ourselves. It's entirely understandable that most of us don't have much time to devote to politics. Besides, what does it really matter?

Well, let's take a look at this, shall we?

Part of the Problem

If we continue to enter politics at the rate we have been, it will be 300 years before there's an equal number of women and men in the Government.

Who's going to write laws that are good for women? We already know the answer. In light of that answer, we really must do more.

'More?' you say.

Yes, I say. I'm not talking about taking on another activity, or running for Parliament (or even the school board), or doing something that will tip us over into the exhaustion that threatens every one of us. I'm talking about using our Inner Bitch to make a better world.

Part of the Solution

The easiest thing to do is to vote with our purse. That's right, don't buy those products whose advertising belittles women, insults us or raises by another notch or two the already unrealistic standards to which we hold ourselves. This takes thought and awareness, and not much time. And if the stores we shop in don't carry products that please us, it's up to us to let them know that, until our needs are met, we'll shop elsewhere.

We can turn off the radio when the offensive disc jockey starts talking.

When there's a candidate worth supporting, we can actually go to one of those fund-raising cocktail parties and we can bring friends.

The next time some elected official who does not serve our needs (we know who they are) sends us a letter asking for money to run again, we can return the letter in the handy pre-addressed envelope with a note saying: 'I don't think so. Not until I see some results from you. For now, I'm donating my money to Oxfam instead.'

The message will be received. Think of it as taking part in a collective 'I don't think so.' Imagine the possibilities.

SHE'S
THE GAL WHO CANNOT ENJOY
THE SWEET TASTE OF SUCCESS.

9 WORK FORCE

**'Power can be taken,
but not given.'**
Gloria Steinem

Work is what we do for money. Money in this society equals power. When we suffer from Toxic Niceness, we fear power. We think it is unattractive.

We may couch this belief in phrases like 'Money's just not important to me,' but it's really that we fear power. Which may explain why, when asked to work more without being paid more, we just say yes.

When we are in touch with our Inner Bitch, we are not afraid of power.

We welcome power.

We also welcome the responsibility that comes with power. We take pride in being good at what we do, and eagerly accept new challenges. We also welcome the money, understanding that it is a manifestation of the energy we put into our work.

We deserve all the rewards that our abilities have won us.

Power

Power begets more power. And power can be used to make changes. Big changes. Little changes.

We all know that, but the question is, 'How do we get power?'

Well, we can be certain no one will hand it to us. Therefore, perhaps the best idea is to make like Lenin, who said, 'I saw power lying in the street and I picked it up.' Look around. Power is at our feet, or maybe on the desk. It may take some looking, given the state of most desks, but we can find it. We see it every day when we open our eyes to it.

Pick it up!

'I don't recognize it,' you say? Here are some traits of power that you may have overlooked:

Teamwork

Power is built on teamwork – think of the Sistine Chapel. Teams are built of individuals. The stronger the individuals, the stronger the team. Toxic Niceness teaches us that being part of a team means agreeing with everything everybody else says. In truth, being part of a team requires that we honestly assess each situation that faces the team and that we speak out about problems or issues.

Imagination

Power comes from imagination. Nothing has ever been created without imagination. No problem has ever been surmounted without imagination. Our Inner Bitch not only puts us in touch with our imagination, She makes us willing to speak up about it. We may not always be right, but being right isn't really the point. Speaking up is. Our contribution may spark an idea in someone else, and that idea might lead to a solution or an invention.

Knowledge

Power is knowledge. And knowledge is power. Each individual has knowledge no one else has. Combining everyone's knowledge begets more knowledge, the way combining rice and beans begets more protein.

How It Works

Every workplace depends on people working together toward a common goal, whether it's serving food, putting out a newspaper, practising law, or whatever. The more power each individual brings to striving for the goal, the more likely it is to be attained.

Toxic Niceness drains us of power. It follows that it also drains power from whatever work we do. We may believe that being nice will get people to do what we want them to do. Nothing could be further from the truth.

Which is not to say that we need to shriek and demand and throw our weight around. No, no, no! Remember – being in touch with our Inner Bitch does not mean that we get to be abusive to anyone. It simply means that we know when to be firm, when to state our position and let it be known that we will act upon our convictions.

Rhymes with Rich

If it's true that you only start being called a bitch when you're successful, then we should embrace the opportunity to be called a bitch in the workplace.

Being called a bitch usually means that we are right or that we are insisting on excellence from others.

According to some people, use of the term 'bitch' has grown in direct proportion to the number of women who have reached the top of their field.

How do we get to the top of our field? We do our job very well, thus advancing to the next level. This usually requires that we work with other people, eventually being in charge of what those other people do.

If we ask those who report to us to do their job well, and that means they have to work harder than they did before, they will probably call us bitch.

If those people who report to us do not do their job and we take them to task for that, they will call us bitch.

If we have taken those people to task and they still do not do their job, we will undoubtedly be more firm with them the second time we talk to them. They will definitely call us bitch.

Good for them. Better for us.

Because what it really means is that we know our business. Here is a simple truth: No matter how nicely we ask, if we are the boss, we are the bitch.

What's the important part of that homily? We are the boss.

Maxine
ACADEMY OF ADVANCED ASSERTIVENESS TRAINING
Quit shovin'!
Get outta my way!
If I wanna butt in line, I'm gonna butt in line!
Oh, yeah? Well, talk to my LAWYER about it!
G#!
Oh, SHUT UP!
Come on, come on! I haven't got all day!
Get outta here!
Gimme that!

10 CLOSE ENCOUNTERS

'We die by comfort and live by conflict.'
May Sarton

It's bound to happen. And although it might sound to the uninitiated like a potential cataclysm, an encounter between two of us who are in touch with our Inner Bitch actually holds the possibility of greatness.

What could be better, after all, than the Inner Bitch doubled? Or tripled, quadrupled, increased exponentially?

Consider this: When two of us in touch with our Inner Bitch meet head on, it's magnetic. We either feel ourselves drawn to each other or we are repelled. Either way, the dynamic that's going on is this: We're recognizing each other's power.

We may not ever become friends with those women whose Inner Bitch we encounter, but that's beside the point. The important thing is, even if we have to agree to disagree, even if we just can't believe the tactics the other woman is using, even if we are filled with envy or some other base emotion, nine times out of ten, the other woman's Inner Bitch will evoke our respect and admiration.

It's better to recognize that confrontation can be exhilarating, that the process of facing off with someone who is as sure of her point of view as you are sure of yours is an opportunity to become more clear. A close encounter with someone else's Inner Bitch is nothing to fear, it's something to welcome.

Perhaps most importantly, there is the potential for great vitality in those interactions where our Inner Bitch meets Her match. It's easy to be with people who agree with us; it's comfortable and dulls our edges. This can be dangerous: Getting along with everyone in our lives gets to be a habit again, and Play Nicely gets a grip on us, beginning the spiral back into Toxic Niceness. Next thing we know, we're apologizing for everything, sitting home on Saturday nights waiting for the phone to ring, and eating the entire cake.

Is this what we want?

APPENDIX A

THE BITCH IN EVERYWOMAN

'I am in the world to change the world.'
Muriel Rukeyser

The Inner Bitch manifests herself in many archetypes. At different moments, your own Inner Bitch may resemble any one of these icons of female power:

Kara The Valkyrie swan queen. Kara overwhelmed her enemies using only the sound of her voice. A bitch to be reckoned with, especially on the phone. She also tells it like it is to her best friends.

Lilith Lilith was to be Adam's first wife, but she took one look at him and said, 'I don't think so'. So off she flew to the banks of the Red Sea, where she spent her days coupling with whomever pleased her, giving birth to hundreds of children every day. Needless to say, with that level of fecundity, some of Lilith's DNA has got to be coursing through each of us.

Catherine De Medici When she married one of those

Kings Louis of France, Catherine brought 18 of her favourite Italian cooks with her. Can you imagine the leftovers? And her home was her castle: She insisted everyone at court use forks to pick up their food, instead of using their fingers. Yes, Mum.

Katharine Hepburn Strong, sassy and ultra-dignified. Never knew that women were supposed to be the inferior sex. Next time you encounter a nasty salesperson, *be* Katharine Hepburn.

Lysistrata A well-known Greek organizer. Persuaded the women of her city-state to withhold sex until the men gave up their most ridiculous war. The key here is that Lys banded together with other like-minded women. Imagine what we could do with the Government.

Buffy the Vampire Slayer She's the head cheerleader and reincarnate vampire slayer. She's in great shape and has a keen fashion sense. Buffy doesn't take any guff.

To bolster your courage as you express that power-packed phrase, 'I don't think so', call upon any one of these great role models, any time.

...AND THE MEN WHO LOVE HER

'Macho does not prove mucho.'
Zsa Zsa Gabor

Just for the record, the idea that we women who are in touch with our Inner Bitch hate men, or wish we were men, or want to be like men, can be summed up with one word – SILLY. I just had to make that point.

No, this chapter is about the men who really admire the women they know who are in touch with their Inner Bitch. We all know men like this – they usually live with our friends. Oh, okay, maybe you actually live with a man like this.

The point is, there's a name for men like this – Prince (as in, 'a Prince among men').

A Prince understands what the Inner Bitch is all about. He gets it.

A Prince Is Not a Wimp

Wimps are those guys who believe that machismo is the highest manifestation of male energy. They are the men who stand us up. The guys who keep dropping the age limit on whom they'll date, until their daughters and their girlfriends are the same age. The guys who won't work for a female boss.

A Prince is a real man, i.e., a real human being.

Who Is a Prince?

Here's how to recognize a Prince:

- ❐ A Prince really does take full responsibility for his share of raising the kids;

- ❐ A Prince understands why those ads for beer are offensive (you know the ones I mean);

- ❐ A Prince never takes it for granted that we'll do all the cooking;

- ❐ Conversely, a Prince does not assume that we can't change a flat tyre;

- ❐ A Prince offers encouragement, rather than advice;

- ❐ A Prince knows what he knows. And, at the same time, he knows what he doesn't know. He doesn't bluster his way through a situation with ever-deepening b.s. In fact, a Prince has a good grasp on just how attractive it really is to be able to say, 'I don't know'.

Where Did He Come From?

Well, if we have an Inner Bitch who is a natural part of us, it must follow that there is also an Inner Prince.

Just as most women have been trained in the ways of Toxic Niceness, men have been trained in the ways of whatever it is they're suffering from. There are plenty of names for it; pick one. Chances are, if you've done your Inner Bitch homework, you won't need to be cruel about it. The point is to understand the dynamic at work here: Men have been taught behaviours that probably run counter to their true natures.

Nature vs. Nurture

My experience has been that it takes a lot of work for a man to become a Prince, but that the basic stuff is there all along.

And try this one on for size: Even the wimpiest, most macho man has the capacity to become a Prince.

Assessing Your Prince Quotient (PQ)

Let's say you are a man who has some inkling about his Inner Prince, and you want to measure just how active this aspect of your being is. Here's a short test:

1 Women like to be called 'girls'.
Agree/Disagree
2 When a woman is assertive, I think of her as a bitch.
Agree/Disagree
3 When I am going somewhere with a woman in a car, I drive.
Always/Most of the time/Seldom/Some of the time/ Whose car are we taking?

4 I know how to do laundry, and iron.
True/False/Why bother? My mum does my laundry.
5 I had an emotional reaction to the movie *Field of Dreams*
True/False/Never saw it

Interpreting Your Answers
Question 1

If you answered 'Agree' and you are under the age of 65, it's a safe bet that you are not a full-fledged Prince. (-10 points)

However, if you based your answer on the fact that your mum and her friends like to be called girls, this reveals a level of sensitivity that implies Princeness. (+2 points)

If you answered 'Disagree', take a moment to reflect on why you chose that response. Is it because women have corrected you for calling them girls? (+2 points)

Or was your answer based on thoughts you've had about the importance of language, and calling women girls is not only inaccurate, but insulting? (+10 points)

Question 2

If you agreed, define 'assertive'. (-10 points if your definitions for men and women are different; +10 if you disagreed)

Question 3

'Whose car is it?' is the question a Prince would ask. (+10)

'Seldom' indicates Princeness only if you own a car. (+7 if you own a car, -10 if you don't)

'Some of the time' seems equitable. (+5)

'Most of the time' may imply that you either drive a large car (conducive to carrying many people or things), or that you have a great car that everyone wants to ride in. (0 points) It may also mean that most of your friends don't own cars. Then you are generous to always drive them around, and we hope your friends pay for petrol. (+10)

If your answer was 'Always', we really do have to look at the reasons why that would be the case. But it doesn't look good for your Prince Quotient. (-10)

Question 4

Okay, this was a sort of trick question, and we won't add or subtract any points for it; I actually don't know how to do laundry. And I'm hopeless at ironing. We threw this one in to see if anyone was paying attention. Of course, if you're in college and your mum does all your laundry, that's just fine.

Question 5

Another trick question – everyone had an emotional reaction to that movie! 'Emotional reaction', after all, covers quite a lot of territory. (0 points; it doesn't matter if you cried or not.) If you didn't see it, you are excused and may take an extra 2 points.

Scoring

If your score was 32 points, you are a full-blown, totally-in-touch Prince.

If your score was 29, you have a high PQ.

19-21 is medium range PQ.

A score of -32 shows a very low PQ. The fact that you took this quiz, however, is a hopeful sign, because awareness is the first step. Don't despair, there is no such thing as a hopeless case. You can improve your PQ.

Getting in Touch with Your Inner Prince

All the things in this book that apply to women getting in touch with our Inner Bitch also apply to men becoming a Prince. To break it down for you:

1 When you sense b.s., don't explain it away – call it as you see it. Even (or maybe particularly) when it is your own b.s.

2 If the desire to act like a wimp (*see above*) is overwhelming, just say to yourself, 'I don't think so. Get a grip, mate.' This works very well, because it bears a striking resemblance to taking the time to respond carefully.

3 Learn the difference between being kind and being patronizing. For example, it is kind to say, 'May I help?' when you see someone struggling to get something done. Like putting two small children to bed. It is patronizing to say 'Y'know, when I put them to bed, I just tuck them in and turn out the light.'

4 Turn up the volume on your internal Prince voice. It's been there all along, whispering to you things like, 'it really is okay to want to spend time with my kids'.

Note: A father spending time with his kids is parenting, not baby-sitting.

5 Recognize that your Inner Prince and my Inner Bitch meet on solid and very even ground.

Solid, even ground is a terrific base upon which to build.

THE 10-MINUTE BITCH

'Success breeds confidence.'
Beryl Markham

These are little things we can do during the day to sharpen reflexes dulled by immersion in Toxic Niceness. As is the case with any sort of exercise, the more we do them, the easier they are. Consider these to be basic training.

The Eye-to-eye Exercise

Stand before a mirror and look yourself in the eye. Think of the last time someone requested something of you that was absurd. For most of us, that would have been within the past 24 hours. Something really silly, like the time your cousin went to India for a month for intensive meditation and asked you to feed her cats every day. In spite of the fact that this required you to drive for an hour, you said yes, didn't you?

Imagine she is asking you to do it again. Hear her voice, see her face. Now smile and say, 'I don't think so, Cousin Menakshi.'

This is especially instructive, because as you remember these absurd requests (whether or not you agreed to them), a pattern may become clear to you. These are the areas where Toxic Niceness is particularly strong in your life. This is important information to have, because awareness is the first step in eradicating unwelcome behaviours.

Voting with Our Purses

Gather together every magazine you have lying around the house. Go through them page by page and rip out any advertisement that offends you. You don't have to justify your being offended, just recognize it. Once you have all those pages gathered (there will probably be a large pile), take them to the store with you the next time you go shopping. Do we want to give those companies our money? I don't think so. Eventually, they will get the message.

I Love Myself; I Think I'm Grand

You know those diet books and articles that you've accumulated over the years?

Destroy them. Each day, rip out a few pages to burn in the sink as you say, 'I am an adult. I choose what I eat.' If you don't think you look great, choose to take reasonable action. We all have enough information about how our bodies actually work; use whatever works for you. Most important, just say 'I don't think so' to the unrealistic ideal everyone else sets for us. Women are supposed to look like people, not scarecrows.

10 Most Wanted

Make a list of all the people who have taken advantage of your immersion in Toxic Niceness. It doesn't matter if they were manipulative, malicious or mean-spirited, because their behaviour is not the point. Yours is. Once a week, pick one of those people and outline for yourself the situation that occurred with that person.

Now, write it the way you wish it had happened, paying specific attention to your behaviour. Don't be afraid; no one else is ever going to see this. The point is this: By rewriting our personal history, we are able to change our present and our future. Knowing what we wish we had done in a situation prepares us for the next time. And there is always a next time.

With a Partner

This is intensive training. Get a friend who really knows your life. Sit facing each other with your feet firmly on the floor, arms relaxed at your sides. Choose one of you to be the receiver, the other the sender. The sender lists all the things to which she wishes she had said, 'I don't think so'. The receiver then repeats the list, giving the sender the chance to say 'I don't think so' out loud.

The receiver throws in a couple of things to which she wishes the sender had said 'I don't think so', like that perm that ruined her hair.

The Power Lullaby

I don't know about you, but the time I spend in bed just before sleep has always been a time of reflection for me. It used to work this way: I'd lie there thinking about all the awful things I'd done, starting when I was in playschool. And I'd beat myself up about those things. In fact, I'd get so upset with myself that I couldn't fall asleep for hours, because one thing led to another and by the time I was drained enough to fall asleep, it was time to get up. Needless to say, I wasn't at my best.

I believe I have found a better way to deal with this reflective time. I think about all the things I have done right in my life. All those times I paid attention to my Inner Bitch, and the times I've pulled myself out of a spiral into Toxic Niceness. I fall asleep with a smile on my face. And when I wake up in the morning, I feel powerful.

Just thought I'd share this with you.

ABOUT THE AUTHOR

Elizabeth Hilts is the editor of an alternative newsweekly. She is a frequent contributor to *Hysteria Magazine* and *Cook's Magazine*. Her work also regularly appears in alternative newspapers throughout the country.

She illuminated the concept of the Inner Bitch for the premiere issue of *Hysteria*, which appeared in February 1993. Her article, titled 'Get In Touch With Your Inner Bitch', was widely reprinted, and Elizabeth was called upon by numerous radio stations to discuss the Inner Bitch on the air.

Eventually, Elizabeth's work came to the notice of Rush Limbaugh, who railed against the Inner Bitch on his radio show for several weeks. Needless to say, he didn't get it.

More to the point was *Elle Magazine's* March 1994 forum, inspired by a reprint of 'Get In Touch With Your Inner Bitch'. Titled 'Yo, Bitch', the forum brought together a group of high-powered women to discuss bitchiness, success, backlash and other topics of importance.

Elizabeth would like to see this book reach every woman who wants to laugh out loud and speak her mind.

Assert Yourself

Gael Lindenfield

Don't spend your life blaming yourself for being inadequate, shy, or too easily led. Learn how to assert yourself!

This best-selling book has already changed the lives of thousands of people. It will show you how to:

- Improve your self-esteem and motivation
- Cope with unfair criticism and exploitation
- Set realistic goals for yourself
- Communicate effectively with others
- Learn from your mistakes
- Stand up for yourself

Gael Lindenfield is the author of the best-selling SUPER CONFIDENCE, SELF ESTEEM and THE POSITIVE WOMAN. She works as a freelance psychotherapist and groupwork consultant and runs successful courses in self-assertiveness and personal development.

'Great for anyone feeling the need for a confidence boost'
TV Times

'Practical, readable and helpful'
Ms London

'A handy guide for building up confidence and acting positively'
Woman's Own

Self Esteem

A complete course in:
• Developing self-worth • Healing emotional wounds
• Breaking self-destructive habits • Building self
esteem in others

Gael Lindenfield

Poor self esteem is at the root of many of our problems. It can sabotage relationships and careers, cause self-destructive behaviour, and can hold us back from achieving our full potential. The beginnings of poor self esteem usually lie far back in our childhoods, but it can be knocked again in our adult life by criticism and trauma.

Gael Lindenfield, best-selling author and leading therapist, has worked with thousands of ordinary people whose lives have dramatically improved after taking her self esteem courses. This book includes practical exercises that you can do in order to help you improve your own self esteem AND that of others.

Use this book to learn how to be:

- Calm, relaxed and confident
- 'At home' with your body
- Self-reliant
- Energetic and purposeful
- Positive and encouraging with children and colleagues

I Want More

Straight-talking advice on how to get what you want

Stephanie Myers

As a black girl growing up with eight brothers and sisters in Bristol, Stephanie Myers learnt from an early age about racial abuse, poverty, unemployment, discrimination and heartache.

With cheerful determination she fought back, and by the age of 26 had formed her own highly successful training company. Her 'tell 'em like it is' approach has helped thousands of people, from teenage ex-offenders to directors of multi-national companies.

In this, her first book, she offers a no-nonsense guide to getting more of what you want – be it respect, job satisfaction, money, confidence or love. No dramatic efforts are required: the key is in small improvements and gradual changes.

If any book can help those struggling against oppression, poverty and unhappiness, then this is it.

The Art of Mingling

Easy, fun and proven techniques for superconfident socializing

Jeanne Martinet

If the thought of entering a room filled with people you don't know makes you go weak at the knees, then this book is what you need.

THE ART OF MINGLING is filled with useful techniques, manoeuvres and ideas to help you feel completely at ease in any kind of party or gathering.

The social success you have always wished for is now within your grasp!

Your Best Year Yet!

A proven method for making the next 12 months your most successful ever

Jinny S Ditzler

This book holds the key to making next year your best ever. After answering the Ten Best Year Yet Questions you will have a simple one-page plan for the next 12 months.

What did I accomplish?
What were my biggest disappointments?
What did I learn?
How do I limit myself and how can I stop?
What are my personal values?
What roles do I play in my life?
What is my major focus for the next year?
What are my goals for each role?
What are my top ten goals for the next year?
How can I make sure I achieve them?

To make new things happen in your life, remember what makes a garden grow. You must first see what's growing now, then pull the weeds, cultivate the soil and water what you've planted before new seeds can flourish. Setting new goals in an unexamined life works no better than tossing seeds into an untended garden.

For over 20 years Jinny Ditzler has been teaching and coaching people to achieve new heights of personal performance. She was the focus of the Channel 4 Programme, 'Executive Coach'.

ASSERT YOURSELF	0 7225 2652 0	£4.99	☐
SELF ESTEEM	0 7225 3017 X	£5.99	☐
I WANT MORE	0 7225 3186 9	£5.99	☐
THE ART OF MINGLING	0 7225 2835 3	£4.99	☐
YOUR BEST YEAR YET!	0 7225 3034 X	£5.99	☐

All these books are available from your local bookseller or can be ordered direct from the publishers.

To order direct just tick the titles you want and fill in the form below:

Name: _____

Address: _____

_____

_____Postcode: _____

Send to: Thorsons Mail Order, Dept 3, HarperCollins*Publishers*, Westerhill Road, Bishopbriggs, Glasgow G64 2QT.
Please enclose a cheque or postal order or your authority to debit your Visa/Access account –

Credit card no: _____

Expiry date: _____

Signature: _____

– to the value of the cover price plus:
UK & BFPO: Add £1.00 for the first book and 25p for each additional book ordered.
Overseas orders including Eire: Please add £2.95 service charge. Books will be sent by surface mail but quotes for airmail despatches will be given on request.

24 HOUR TELEPHONE ORDERING SERVICE FOR ACCESS/VISA CARDHOLDERS – TEL: 0141 772 2281.